THE INVISIBLE GOVERNMENT

THE INVISIBLE GOVERNMENT

GEORGE A. LeROY

Belleville, Ontario, Canada

THE INVISIBLE GOVERNMENT

Copyright © 2005, George A. LeRoy

All Scripture quotations, unless otherwise specified, are from *The Holy Bible, King James Version.* Copyright © 1977, 1984, Thomas Nelson Inc., Publishers. • Scripture quotations marked TLB are taken from *The Living Bible.* Copyright © 1971 by Tyndale House Publishers, Wheaton, Illinois 60187. All rights reserved. • *Weymouth New Testament.* Copyright © 1912 by James Clarke & Co., London. • *The James Moffat Translation of the Bible.* Copyright © 1934 by Hodder and Stoughton Limited, London.

Library and Archives Canada Cataloguing in Publication

Leroy, George, 1932-

The invisible government / George LeRoy.

Includes bibliographical references.

ISBN 1-55306-988-9
ISBN 1-55306-990-0 (LSI ed.)

1. Spiritual warfare--Biblical teaching. I. Title.

BT975.L47 2005   235'.4   C2005-905831-5

**To contact the author
for more information, see:**

Web site at: www.areyoubound.com
E-mail at:revgeog@aol.com

Guardian Books is an imprint of *Essence Publishing,* a Christian Book Publisher dedicated to furthering the work of Christ through the written word.. For more information, contact:

20 Hanna Court, Belleville, Ontario, Canada K8P 5J2
Phone: 1-800-238-6376 • Fax: (613) 962-3055
E-mail: publishing@essencegroup.com
Internet: www.essencegroup.com

DEDICATION

I t is with deep appreciation that I dedicate this book to my wife Ruth, who, as a believer in the Lord Jesus Christ, has been a great influence on my life through her love and total commitment to Jesus Christ. We have learned in our walk with the Lord that "*all things work together for good to them that love God, to them who are the called according to his purpose* (Romans 8:28).

I also wish to thank Deborah Lynn, my daughter, for her help in transcribing the original pages, which desperately needed her loving touch! Many hours were needed to bring it to a satisfactory conclusion. At times she would tell me, "You're not finished yet." Now I am!

To my grandchildren—Becky, Kylah, Tyler and Dee Dee—my prayer is that they will continue to prepare and work out their own salvation (rescue) by continuing to allow the Holy Spirit to work within them and that they will learn to follow His leading in whatsoever state they find themselves. They are very dear to my heart and to the heart of their Lord and Saviour Jesus Christ.

I thank God, through Jesus Christ my Lord, for His love and faithfulness in showing me the way into all truth! *"I therefore so run, not as uncertainly; so fight I, not as one that beateth the air. But I keep under my body, and bring it into subjection: lest that by any means, when I have preached to others, I myself should be a castaway* [unapproved; unworthy]"
(1 Corinthians 9:26-27).

Special thanks to my very good friends Joe, Mary and Luigi, for their contribution towards the publishing of this book.

I would also like to thank Joel Robert for his fabulous graphic interpretations on the cover and throughout the book and his wife, Karen, for her keen eye to editing details.

Note: Please refer to the glossary at the back of the book for several word definitions.

INTRODUCTION

As I sit down to begin this major undertaking of sharing my understanding and experiences of the spirit world, I am overwhelmed, knowing my limitations in expressing in a basic, practical and understandable way the knowledge I have of this realm.

In my pastoral ministry over the years, many questions and situations arose when I had no understanding of how to address them and bring complete victory when necessary. To address spiritual problems with natural methods is one thing. Many have tried and failed. To address spiritual problems with spiritual methods is quite another!

As spiritual understanding came to me through my years as a pastor, evangelist and teacher, it became quite clear that I was in a war with an enemy who had one objective. That objective is "*to steal, to kill and to destroy*" (John 10:10), fully hindering God's plan of "*bringing* [leading] *many sons unto* [indicating the point reached] *glory* [as very apparent, dignity]" (Hebrews 2:10).

The knowledge received from the Lord through the Spirit has enabled me in the past few years to understand and deal more fully with the spiritual situations I have been confronted with and to bring victory out of what had seemed defeat in these situations. I believe that as you read you will find many answers to the many questions and situations you, no doubt, have encountered concerning your spiritual walk.

Allow me at this point to quote Ephesians 6:12:

> *For we wrestle not against flesh and blood, but against principalities, against powers, against the rulers of the dark-ness of this world, against spiritual wickedness in high places.*

> *For we are not fighting against people made of flesh and blood, but against persons without bodies – the evil Kings of the unseen world, those mighty satanic beings and great evil princes of darkness who rule this world; and against huge numbers of wicked spirits in the spirit world* (TLB).

For we have to struggle not with blood and flesh but with the angelic rulers, the angelic authorities, the potentates of the dark present, the spirit – forces of evil in the heavenly sphere (The James Moffat Translation of the Bible).

For ours is not a conflict with mere flesh and blood, but with the despotisms, the empires, the forces that control and govern this dark world—the spiritual hosts of evil arrayed against us in the heavenly warfare (Weymouth New Testament).

For our fight is not against any physical enemy: it is against organisations and powers that are spiritual. We are up against the unseen power that controls this dark world, and spiritual agents from the very headquarters of evil (J.B. Phillips).

Let us look now at the *Invisible Government.* Let us address the questions we have and come to understand how to find the answers and gain victory through...*knowing your enemy*!

THE INVISIBLE GOVERNMENT

We are told in the Bible, *"And we know that we are of God, and the whole world lieth in wickedness"* [is under Satan's power and control] (1 John 5:19).

Questions naturally arise:
- How did this happen?
- Why did this happen?

To answer these questions, we must first believe that God exists, and also the devil; and secondly, we must believe in good and evil. The purpose of this writing is not to prove either but assumes the reader believes both and will continue on and read without prejudice what is written in these pages.

We know and understand from the Bible

that *"Yes, all have sinned; all fall short of God's glorious ideal"* (Romans 3:23, TLB). *"Everyone has sinned, everyone falls short of the beauty of God's plan"* (Romans 3:23, J.B. Phillips). *"For all have sinned, and come short of the glory of God"* (Romans 3:23).

We also read in the Bible, *"For the wages of sin is death"*(Romans 6:23). *"Sin pays its servants: the wage is death"* (Romans 6:23, J.B. Phillips).

We all know death is certain! Whatever you think regarding the Bible and sin, death is a certainty – the "wages" of sin.

(Figure 1)

This, then, is what happened. Sin made its entry into the world through one man, and through sin, death. The entail of sin and death passed on to the whole human race, and no one could break it for no one was himself free from sin (Romans 5:12, J.B. Phillips).

"Nevertheless death, the complement of sin, held sway over mankind from Adam to Moses, even over those whose sin was quite unlike Adam's" (Romans 5:14, J.B. Phillips).

What we have then, is a world, with all its inhabitants, controlled by an *Invisible Government* producing spiritual pollution.

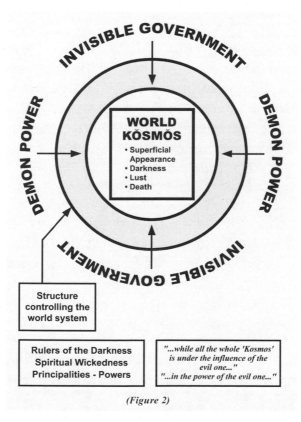

(Figure 2)

Understanding Darkened - *Being alienated from the life of God through the ignorance that is in them because of the blindness of their heart.*

- *Matthew 12:34*
- *Matthew 15:18-19*
- *Mark 7:23*
- *Luke 6:45*

(Figure 3)

"O generation of vipers, how can ye, being evil, speak good things? for out of the abundance of the heart the mouth speaketh" (Matthew 12:34). *Abundance* means "surplus or superabundance, to be in excess." *Of the heart* means "the thoughts or feelings" (mind) (see Fig. 3), also (by analogy) "the middle."

> *But these things which proceed out of the mouth come forth from the heart, and they defile the man. For out of the heart proceed evil thoughts, murders, adulteries, fornications, thefts, false witness, and blasphemies* (Matthew 15: 18-19). (Compare to Mark 7:21-22.)

"All these evil things come from within [from inside; inwardly], *and defile* [pollute] *the man"* (Mark 7:23).

> *A good man out of the good treasure of his heart bringeth forth that which is good; and an evil [in effect or influence] man out of the evil treasure [theasurôs] of his heart bringeth forth that which is evil: for of the abundance of the heart his mouth speaketh* (Luke 6:45).

It was Paul the Apostle who said, *"So I run straight to the goal with purpose in every step. I fight to win. I'm not just shadow-boxing or playing around"* (1 Corinthians 9:26, TLB). We now know there is an invisible enemy who creates havoc with and in our lives. We believe we are in control of everything we say and do, yet in reality, through our experiences, find that is not true.

We have often heard how someone "fights their own demons." They certainly are using the right terminology; yet do they really believe they are demons? If so, what can they do to rid themselves of them?

We *must* realize that *"The heart* [used figuratively very widely for the feelings, the will and the intellect, likewise for the centre of anything] *is deceitful* [polluted] *above all things, and desperately wicked* [incurable, sick]: *who can know* [to ascertain by seeing, including observation] *it?"* (Jeremiah 17:9).

Once sin made its entry into the world, the enemy then proceeded to make inroads into our lives as an organized power and then operated through the members of our body.

When Cain, due to certain circumstances, became angry and jealous of his brother Abel, he still had the opportunity to change his attitude. Instead of doing this, he allowed the enemy to penetrate his life, and he murdered his brother Abel. He was now captive to a spirit of murder as well as anger and jealousy.

Our hearts are filled with the spirits of the world because of the yielding of the members of our bodies to the enemy. I recall praying with a young man who had a spirit of rape. The spirit troubled this young man only at times. Certain situations would arise to become the catalysts to generate an overpowering sexual urge to rape the individual at hand. Once the act had been done, the spirit of rape retreated, only to reappear at another time. *If* the young man had not received deliverance, this spirit in him would have become stronger, and he would, no doubt, have become a serial rapist. The more we yield to whatever spirit(s) we have—whether fornication, lust, anger, lying, etc.—the stronger the spirit(s) become. Eventually other spirits, more wicked, will enter into our lives and will bring greater bondage(s) to our lives.

The following illustration will explain how spirits exercise their power, desires and characteristics.

Spirit of Lust (sexual): Hidden until something or someone becomes the catalyst to generate the urge to fulfill the desire.

(A)	When activated, this overpowering desire (urge) rises up to block out any restraints raised against such an action, therefore, committing the act!

(B)	When the desire is satisfied, the spirit returns to its original place until another situation arises at another time.

How many times have you heard someone say, "I don't know why I did it" or "something just took hold of me"? Think of the Holocaust and the atrocities committed in the concentration camps by individuals who were supposed to be civilized human beings. Medical doctors performing scientific operations on unsuspecting children, causing untold suffering and torture. Adults and children were used for medical experiments, supposedly for the advancement of scientific discovery. Gas chambers were used to wipe out millions of people, all because of hate, jealousy and anti-Semitic views.

WHY? WHY? WHY?

DEMON POWER IS IN CONTROL OF THIS WORLD!

Demons take civilized human beings and change them into the perverted evil of the spirit world. Remember, in certain cases, an individual knows what is right and wrong but has this irresistible, overpowering impulse (urge) that renders choice impossible.

We see the effects of "spiritual pollution" everywhere. The miasma (noxious atmosphere) from the spirit world endeavours to pollute as much of humankind as possible. These putrefying spirits, in invisible form, penetrate human life through temptation, capturing and bringing into bondage those who succumb to the temptation(s).

We read how the tempter (Satan) took Jesus to a very high mountain, showed Him all the kingdoms of the world and their magnificence, and said, *"Everything there I will give you...if you will fall down and worship me"* (Matthew 4:8-9, J.B. Phillips).

We know Satan tempted Jesus in three areas: the lust of the eye, the lust of the flesh and the pride of life. We also know Jesus did not succumb (yield) to the temptations! Why?

We find the answer in Luke's Gospel. *"And Jesus being full of the Holy Ghost returned from Jordan, and was led by the Spirit into the wilderness"* (Luke 4:1). God had given to Jesus, through the Holy Spirit, power to withstand the temptations of the enemy (Satan), thus setting an example to all of us of the possibility of living a righteous life if we trust and obey. All through His life, Jesus relied solely on the Holy Spirit to lead and guide Him.

We read in John 5: 19 and 30,

Then answered Jesus and said unto them, Verily, verily, I say unto you, The Son can do nothing of himself, but what he seeth the Father do: for what things soever he doeth, these also doeth the Son likewise...I can of mine own self do nothing."

Although temptations came to Jesus, He trusted the Holy Spirit within Him to constantly overcome the enemy, therefore remaining sinless!

We read, when the time came for Jesus to go to the cross, *"Hereafter I will not talk much with you; for the prince of this world cometh, and hath nothing in me"* (John 14:30). Jesus had conquered the enemy (Satan) and would after the resurrection give to us the power to become (to cause to be, generate, come into being) sons of God. God had ordained this before the world, unto our glory. If Satan had known God's plan, he would never have crucified the Lord of Glory! Now Satan, through his *Invisible Government*, is hindering as much as possible, to stop God's plan from being fulfilled. We are the objects of Satan's attacks.

We must know our enemy and see the world for what it is. Remember, the whole world system is controlled by a structured *Invisible Government* operating through man's fallen nature, primitive desires, greedy ambitions and the glamour of all that man thinks is splendid.

Oh, what delusion and deception Satan has brought to humankind!

Insight into and knowledge of what and who we are fighting will help us in our understanding the questions we have concerning our own emotions, desires and ultimately our actions.

We read in Mark 7:20-23,

> *"It is the thought-life that pollutes for from within, out of men's hearts, come evil thoughts of lust, theft, murder, adultery, wanting what belongs to others, wickedness, deceit, lewdness, envy, slander, pride, and all other folly. All these vile things come from within"* (Mark 7:20-23, TLB).

"In whom the god of this world hath blinded the minds of them which believe not" (2 Corinthians 4:4).

Having briefly looked at the enemy's position in and over the earth (Kôsmôs), we must now address another "realm" (God's) and understand how we can *have victory over our enemy instead of defeat!*

> *And what is the exceeding greatness of his power to us-ward who believe, according to the working of his mighty power, Which he wrought in Christ, when he raised him from the dead, and set him at his own right hand in the heavenly places, Far above all principality, and*

power, and might, and dominion, and every name that is named, not only in this world, but also in that which is to come (Ephesians 1: 19-21).

CHRIST
Far Above All Principality & Power & Might & Dominion

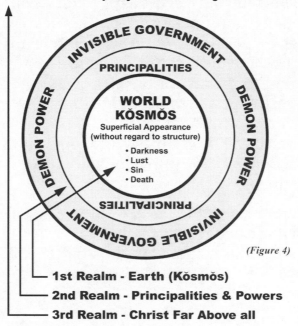

(Figure 4)

1st Realm - Earth (Kŏsmŏs)
2nd Realm - Principalities & Powers
3rd Realm - Christ Far Above all

And how tremendous is the power available to us who believe in God. That power is the same divine energy which was demonstrated in Christ when he raised him from the dead and gave him the place of highest honour in Heaven— a place that is infinitely superior to any

*command, authority, power or control;
and which carries with it a name far
beyond any name that could ever be
used in this world or the world to come"*
(Ephesians 1: 19-21, J.B. Phillips).

You, as well as I, know in practice what happens in our everyday living. Our own behaviour astounds and baffles us. We find ourselves not doing what we really want to do and, many times, doing what we really hate. We often find that we have the will to do good but not the power to accomplish it. The evil we really don't want to do we find ourselves doing. We are slaves, servants, and obey and yield our members to uncleanness and tools of wickedness!

- What a terrible mess we find ourselves in!
- Where will we find help?
- Who will free us from this battle within?
- We are at war within ourselves!
- Who will free us from the bondage within?

"I thank God through Jesus Christ our Lord" (Romans 7:25).

"I thank God there is a way out through Jesus Christ our Lord" (J.B. Phillips).

*You were spiritually dead through your
sins and failures, all the time that you
followed this world's ideas of living, and
obeyed the evil ruler of the spiritual*

realm—who is indeed fully operative today in those who disobey God. We all lived like that in the past, and followed the desires and imaginings of our lower nature, like everyone else (Ephesians 2:1-3, J.B. Phillips).

You went along with the crowd and were just like all the others, full of sin, obeying Satan, the mighty prince of the power of the air, who is at work right now in the hearts of those who are against the Lord (Ephesians 2:2-3, TLB).

We would like, if possible, to confront, examine and find the answer to the question of how and what we can do to rid, expel, send away our own personal demons. I am sure that many or all of us know those things within that overcome us at certain times in our lives. Many of us wear a mask—a facade—before others as an outward appearance yet fight a war within! How many babies at the time of their birth are murderers, molesters, adulterers, fornicators, liars, racists, thieves, etc.? What is it, over time, that causes such radical changes of behaviour in the lives of many of these individuals?

For example, I met a family that had four children, three girls and one boy. Over the years, one daughter became a lesbian; another daughter got involved in crime; another daughter was very promiscuous; and the son died of leukemia at a young age. Mother and father had their own personal issues throughout their marriage, creating an unstable family life. We know through environment, family, life relationships, etc., much can happen that changes an individual for good or bad.

We read in the Living Bible,

> *If you are wise, live a life of steady goodness, so that only good deeds will pour forth. And if you don't brag about them, then you will be truly wise! And by all means, don't brag about being wise and good if you are bitter and jealous and selfish; that is the worst sort of lie. For jealousy and selfishness are not God's kind of wisdom. Such things are earthly, unspiritual, inspired by the devil* (James 3:13-16).)

For wherever there is jealousy or selfish ambition, there will be disorder and every kind of evil. Another way of saying it is,

> *For where envying [jealousy] and strife [quarrelling; contention; stimulate to anger; provoke; intrigue; a plot or scheme usually complicated and intended to effect some purpose by secret schemes, designs, ingenious devices; bad, etc.] is, there is confusion [instability; disorder; commotion] and every evil [foul or flawed; defect made by violence] work*

[deed; action; achievement; feat; accomplishment] (James 3:16).

Remember what we have already said,

For we are not fighting against people made of flesh and blood, but against persons without bodies—the evil rulers of the unseen world, those mighty satanic beings and great evil princes of darkness who rule this world; and against huge numbers of wicked spirits in the spirit world (Ephesians 6:12, TLB).

Some years ago, I prayed with a young man who was full of rebellion. He hated any and all kinds of authority and therefore was consistently finding himself in all kinds of trouble. As a child, whenever he got into trouble, his father would discipline him in an extremely harsh and severe manner. After his last disciplinary beating, he promised himself he would never cry again and would do whatever he wanted. He went outside that day and started to swing on the swings outside. Suddenly he felt a presence that entered his body. He told me he felt extremely strong, and from then on his life changed from bad to very bad. The spirit of rebellion had entered his life, and over the years, trouble and violence were his companions. Prison became his reward until AIDS took his life at an early age.

In one of my teaching seminars, I met a pastor's wife who grew up believing she could not trust any man. Her mother, because of her own issues, had repeatedly told her daughter to never fully trust any man. The daughter, now a pastor's wife, didn't want her husband praying with or for any women in the church. When her husband did, major marital problems occurred in the home and much dissension permeated the church.

We all know evangelists, pastors, priests and other religious leaders who become victims to their own demons, thinking there is no answer. They battle and struggle within themselves, trying to overcome, yet in the end succumb to the overwhelming desire within and end up defeated and guilt ridden.

I know of one pastor who was told by the board of his church to pastor the whole church (all the families), not just the men. His wife would become insanely jealous if he counselled any of the women. This, of course, caused him untold emotional stress and pastoral difficulties. He later resigned the pastorate, not realizing there was an answer to this problem.

Children or adults caught in an act of breaking the law fear the repercussions, punishment, etc., and many times will lie rather than tell the truth. Entrance will be given to a spirit of lying and fear of punishment. This then will produce greater bondage within their lives.

I prayed with a mother who had birthed thirteen children. One child died at birth, but she raised the twelve living children. As all mothers who have raised a family know, all children have different personalities. As a mother she was faced with awesome responsibilities, and over the years, she became discouraged and emotionally stressed out. Many stressful situations arose in her struggle to raise the children. After a particularly difficult day, the thought came to her mind to walk out of the house and commit suicide. At other times she became ill. Through all of these negative experiences, a spirit of death entered her body. Knowing absolutely nothing about spiritual warfare, this spirit remained hidden in her life until God in His mercy exposed this entity.

I became this woman's pastor and one afternoon received a phone call to pray for her, as she was very ill. I prayed for her healing over the telephone, but no relief came. I then visited her home, and when I walked in, she was lying on the living room couch. I looked at her and immediately knew she was dying. I turned to her teenage son standing in the doorway and told him to call an ambulance. I knelt in front of this lady and asked her to explain to me what she was experiencing in her body. As she began to explain, a masculine voice suddenly spoke through her, saying, "I have tried to kill her twice, and this time I will."

The Lord spoke to me through His Spirit and said, "Cast out the spirit of death." After a brief spiritual battle, the woman was delivered. The ambulance arrived a few moments later and took her to the hospital, where she passed kidney stones in a urine specimen. She was released from the hospital a few hours later. This lady is still living today and, I might say, is enjoying life.

There are many others I have prayed with who have had bondages in their lives, such as lying, anger, lust, recklessness, stealing, lewdness, inhibitions, etc. I remember one individual who had the spirit of sloth (slothfulness). He related to me how he never really applied himself to anything he did. He told me he did just enough to get by. After we prayed and he was set free from this slothful spirit, his life completely changed. He is very successful today.

There are those who will tell you there are no answers to the problems we face in society today. I believe there is an answer to all the problems we face!

Be careful that nobody spoils your faith through intellectualism or high-sounding nonsense. Such stuff is at best founded on men's ideas of the nature of the world and disregards Christ! (Colossians 2:8, J.B. Phillips).

Don't let others spoil your faith and joy with their philosophies, their wrong and shallow answers built on men's thoughts and ideas, instead of on what Christ has said (Colossians 2:8, TLB).

Don't you realize that you can choose your own Master? You can choose sin [death] or else obedience [with acquittal]. The one to whom you offer yourself—he will take you and be your master and you will be his slave (Romans 6:16, TLB).

Remember—none of us can look at someone else and know what is in the heart of that person or what they battle within. How many times have you heard, read or said, "He doesn't look like a rapist (a molester, a murderer)," or "She would never kill her own children," etc.

Have you ever heard someone say, "I don't know why I did it?" There is an answer for society's ills if we will acknowledge there is a God who loves us and is willing to help us, if we accept His terms.

Many women today give birth to children while not realizing that their emotional state at the time of conception will have some effect on the baby's personality. If the mother, at any time through the pregnancy, tries to abort the fetus and is not successful, a spirit of death will enter the unborn child and will manifest itself in the individual's life through a serious illness or disease.

I remember praying with a race-car driver who had a spirit of death in him. This young man loved to live on the edge, because he was adventuresome (bold, daring, incurring hazard) and not cognizant of the spirit world around him. This allowed a spirit of recklessness and death to enter his body. Through the grace of God, this young man was completely freed of these spirits and is doing well today.

How many times have you heard or read of skydivers falling to their deaths or of serious race-car crashes where the driver narrowly escaped death? We then hear people say, "These things will happen," or "Accidents are bound to happen."

An accident is an event that takes place without one's foresight or expectation, an event that proceeds from an unknown cause. I certainly disagree with this definition! Why? We read,

> Be careful—watch out for attacks from Satan your great enemy. He prowls around like a hungry, roaring lion, looking for some victim to tear apart" (1 Peter 5:8, TLB).

Some might say, "If I believe what you are saying, I will live in a state of fear or apprehension of some impending or expected evil." Not at all! We read in Proverbs 1:33, "But all who listen to me shall live in peace and safety, unafraid"

(TLB). Also, *"Thou wilt keep him in perfect peace, whose mind is stayed on thee: because he trusteth in thee"* (Isaiah 26:3).

Fear, depression, rejection, shyness, abandonment, and insecurity are only some of the emotional problems women can have through their pregnancies that sometimes can and will affect the fetus. I prayed for a young man who had a strong spirit of lust. He shared with me that he had never been involved with any immoral activity. After much discussion, I discovered his mother had been involved, while married, with another man. Many serious problems had arisen through this affair, and the result was this young man was born with a strong lust spirit.

There was a young woman whose marriage was in serious trouble due to her promiscuity. This woman had, for as long as she could remember, a strong sex drive. Through counselling we found out her mother had been a prostitute, and she was an illegitimate child. She then was raised in this lascivious environment, and because of this, strong spirits of lust penetrated her young life. In her adolescence and later in her married life, these spirits of lust manifested and caused her severe problems. Strife, confusion and divorce were the ultimate outcome in her marriage.

Pornography (child or adult), as we know, is very prevalent in our society and causes serious problems that many individuals are ignorant of. Once we have participated, through seeing or reading it, we immediately allow an opening for the spirit of pornography and the spirit of fantasies and imaginations to infiltrate our lives. Pornography brings sexual stimulation, and the spirit of fantasies and imaginations generate the desire to act out in reality the ideas or notions and pictures that fill the mind. We know that molestation, incest, rape and murder can be the ultimate result of watching or reading pornographic material.

Remember, we are wrestling—warring— against the spirit world!

An evangelist who as a young child read pornographic magazines certainly did not realize that through doing this he would be infiltrated by a lustful, evil, depraved and perverted spirit. Later on, at some point in his life, this spirit became active. He succumbed or yielded to the strong lustful urge and fulfilled the desire within him by visiting with a prostitute. The revelation of what he had done was made known to the public. This brought shame and public embarrassment to himself, his family and his ministry.

I prayed for a young man who had a faker spirit. This spirit endeavours to deceive by furnishing something spurious (false, not legitimate) as though genuine or legitimate. This young man would go to work, fake an accident or sickness, and then get sent home. After hearing about the message of deliverance, he confessed, and this spirit was cast out. He now does an honest day's work for an honest day's pay. How great God is!

"The thief's [Satan's] *purpose is to steal, kill and destroy. My purpose is to give life in all its fullness"* (John 10:10, TLB). I prayed for an Italian mother's son who had a spirit of witchcraft. The mother's father had brought a warlock to her home while she was pregnant. The warlock laid his hands on her stomach and told her, "This boy will have my power." The mother, at this point, did not even know what gender her baby was. She also did not believe what the warlock said to her. A few years later, to her amazement, her son needed to be delivered of the spirit of witchcraft.

There are individuals who are very interested in magic. To me, magic is the supposed art of putting into action the power of spirits. This, I am sure, is an oversimplification of what magic is; yet, I believe that the spirit world becomes very much involved.

There are many names given, such as, *sorcery, enchantment, necromancy, conjuring, black arts, legerdemain* (sleight of hand), *jugglery, witchery, enchantment,* etc. Whatever name is given, all of it encompasses and involves the spirit world. My advice to you is to stay away from all of it.

We are given good advice from God's word. We are told

> There shall not be found among you any one that maketh his son or his daughter to pass through the fire, or that useth divination, or an observer of times, or an enchanter, or a witch. Or a charmer, or a consulter with familiar spirits, or a wizard, or a necromancer (Deuteronomy 18: 10-11).

Why? Because all who do these things are an abomination unto the Lord.

We see, today, individuals who have familiar spirits that are supposed to come when called. These are nothing more than demons—evil spirits! People are captivated by individuals who profess to have a special gift of talking with someone's dead relative, be it mother, father, son, daughter, etc. They supposedly tell people about future things, such as changing jobs, moving to another city, etc. All of this involves demon power and opens individuals to the spirit world.

When we visit a physician, we are asked about our family history. Is there cancer, diabetes and other such diseases in our family? We know these diseases can be passed on through birth. If it can happen in the natural, it can also happen in the spiritual (e.g., lying, stealing, rebellion, anger, lust, etc.).

A mother, because of negative circumstances may not want the baby she is pregnant with. When the baby is born, that child can have a spirit of rejection. A family member came with such a spirit. Because the pregnancy was not wanted, her mother rejected her while she was in the womb. She always felt rejected until that spirit was cast out.

Remember figure 4, the chart showing three realms? We now want to look at the third realm again, as we have only touched on it briefly.

> *And how tremendous is the power available to us who believe in God. That power is the same divine energy which was demonstrated in Christ when he raised him from the dead and gave him the place of highest honour in Heaven— a place that is infinitely superior to any command, authority, power or control; and which carries with it a name far beyond any name that could ever be used in this world or the world to come* (Ephesians 1:19-21, J.B. Phillips).

We are told that *"The thief's purpose is to steal, kill and destroy. My purpose is to give life in all its fullness"*(John 10:10, TLB). Once we believe that Jesus Christ, God's Son, is the answer we have been looking for; we are on our way to a life lived in *victory*!

For He has rescued us out of darkness and gloom of Satan's kingdom and brought us into the kingdom of His dear Son, who bought our freedom with His blood and forgave us all our sins (Colossians 1:13, TLB).

In Acts 2:38-39 we read,

Then Peter said unto them, Repent [think differently; reconsider morally; feel guilty], and be baptized every one of you in the name of Jesus Christ for [assigning a reason; used in argument, explanation] the remission [dismissal; release] of sins, and ye shall receive the gift [present; free gift] of the Holy Ghost. For the promise is unto you, and to your children, and to all that are afar off, even as many as the LORD our God shall call.

Repent—change your views and purpose to accept the will of God in your inner selves instead of rejecting it. And as an expression of it, let every one of you be baptized in the name of Jesus Christ, that you may have your sins forgiven (remission); then you also shall receive the gift the Holy Spirit.

We see all around us the validation of the Bible!

In 2 Timothy 3:2-5 it says,

> *For people will love only themselves and their money; they will be proud and boastful, sneering at God, disobedient to their parents, ungrateful to them, and thoroughly bad. They will be hard-headed and never give in to others; they will be constant liars and troublemakers and will think nothing of immorality. They will be rough and cruel, and sneer at those who try to be good. They will betray their friends; they will be hot-headed, puffed up with pride, and prefer good times to worshipping God. They will go to church; yes, but they won't really believe anything they hear* (TLB).

We have seen secularism, a supposed ethical system founded on natural morality, given supreme attention in the affairs of this life, to the exclusion of religious or sacred influences. It is the promotion of worldliness or the love of the world with the ultimate goal of having the inhabitants of the earth (humanity) devoted entirely to worldly pursuits.

This is absolutely contrary to what the Lord tells us in 1 John 2:15-16:

> *Stop loving this evil world and all that it offers you, for when you love these things you show that you do not really*

love God. For all these worldly things, these evil desires—the craze for sex, the ambition to buy everything that appeals to you, and the pride that comes from wealth and importance— these are not from God. They are from this evil world itself (TLB).

It was the Greek philosopher Aristippus who taught that pleasure, or the gratification of natural desires, was the only conceivable object in life. We know it as *hedonism* (science of pleasure or positive enjoyment). It was George Washington who said, "Reason and experience both forbid us to expect that natural morality can prevail in exclusion of religious principles" (*Webster's New Dictionary*, p. 1093).

It was Isaiah who said, *"They say that what is right is wrong, and what is wrong is right; that black is white and white is black; bitter is sweet and sweet is bitter"* (Isaiah 5:20, TLB). This is happening now and will only intensify in the days to come.

The *Invisible Government* that surrounds us continues to infiltrate our lives, and the Holy Spirit tells us

that in the last times some in the church will turn away from Christ and become eager followers of teachers with devil-inspired ideas. These teachers will tell lies with straight faces and do it so often that their consciences won't even bother them" (1Timothy 4:1-2, TLB).

Today is the time

when people won't listen to the truth, but will go around looking for teachers who will tell them just what they want to hear. They won't listen to what the Bible says but will blithely follow their own misguided ideas (2 Timothy 4:3-4, TLB).

I cannot help but think of another Scripture that says,

"Before every man there lies a wide and pleasant road that seems right but ends in death. Laughter cannot mask a heavy heart. When the laughter ends, the grief remains (Proverbs 14:12-13, TLB).

Satan is an extremely good liar!

Look around at the outcome of his selling abilities. Jails, hospitals and psychiatric institutions are full of individuals who accepted his lies, and even today we ignore what we see and continue to believe him. A fool thinks he needs no advice, but a wise man listens to others (see Proverbs 12:15, TLB).

In Romans 1:16-32 we read,

For I am not ashamed of this good news about Christ. It is God's powerful method of bringing all who believe it to heaven. This message was preached first to the Jews alone, but now everyone is invited to come to God in this same way. This good news tells us that God makes us ready for heaven—makes us right in God's sight. When we put our faith and trust in Christ to save us. This is accomplished from start to finish by faith. As the scripture says it, "the man who finds life will find it through trusting God." But God shows his anger from heaven against all sinful, evil men who push away the truth from them. For the truth about God is known to them instinctively [literally, "is manifest in them]. God has put the knowledge in their hearts. Since earliest times, men have seen the earth and sky and all God made, and have known of His existence and great eternal power. So they will have no excuse when they stand before God at judgment day. Yes, they knew about Him all right, but they wouldn't admit it or worship Him or even thank Him for all his daily care. After awhile, they began to think up silly ideas of what God was like and what He wanted them to do. The result was that their foolish minds became dark and confused. Claiming themselves to be wise without God, they became utter fools instead. And then, instead of worshiping the glorious, ever-living God, they took wood and stone and made idols for themselves, carving them to look like mere birds and animals and snakes and puny men. So God let them go ahead into every sort of sex sin and do whatever they wanted to—yes, vile and sinful things with each other's bodies. Instead of believing what they knew was the truth about God; they deliberately chose to believe lies. So they prayed to the things God made, but wouldn't obey the blessed God who made these things. That is why God let go of them and let them do all these evil things, so that even their women turned against God's natural plan for them and indulged in sex sin with each other. And the men, instead of having a normal sex relationship with women, burned with lust for each other, men doing shameful things with other men and, as a result, getting paid within their own souls with the penalty they so richly deserved. So it was that when they gave God up and would not even acknowledge Him, God gave them up to doing everything their evil minds could think of. Their lives became full of every kind of wickedness and sin, of greed and hate, envy, murder, fighting, lying, bitterness and gossip. They were backbiters, haters of God, insolent, proud braggarts, always thinking of new ways of sinning and continually being disobedient to their parents. They tried to misunderstand, broke their promises and were heartless - without pity. They were fully aware of God's death penalty for these crimes, yet they went right ahead and did them anyway and encouraged others to do them too (TLB).

"My, oh my! What terrible people you have been talking about! I'm not like them!" Yes, you are. Do you think that God will judge and condemn others for doing these things and overlook you when you do them too? All of us know right from wrong. God's laws are written within; our conscience accuses us or sometimes excuses us.

"One day, God is going to judge the secret lives of everyone, their inmost thoughts and motives, this is all part of God's great plan" (TLB). We can say within ourselves, "I don't care"; yet we all know a comment such as this will not change what God has said! We can argue and say when we do wrong, "The devil makes us do it, and it isn't our fault!" *Not so!*

If we believe in the devil and believe it's his fault, then we must adjust our mindset and believe that God through Christ has made a way of escape for us. We need help in this battle against the demonic forces arrayed against us. We need spiritual help in this spiritual battle. Remember, we are not wrestling against flesh and blood but against persons without bodies— the evil rulers of the unseen world, the *Invisible Government* (see Ephesians 6:12).

Our problems or issues are within us! For from the heart come evil thoughts (see Mark 7:21). We understand the *heart*, figuratively speaking, means the thoughts or feelings (mind) and also, by analogy, the middle. This now brings us to the illustration of the man with the two circles in his heart (middle).

The circle with the snake represents how *the Invisible Government* has penetrated our lives with evil, depending on our birth, growth, environment, family life, education, etc. We know everyone is different. How we conduct our lives and what effect we have on humanity depends most certainly on the above mentioned factors (e.g., birth, growth, environment, etc.).

Through our living, we yield ourselves to the many scenarios of life—good or bad—that we are confronted with.

> *"Don't you realize that you can choose your own master? You can choose sin [with death] or else obedience [with acquittal]. The one to whom you offer yourself, he will take you and be your*

master and you will be his slave"
(Romans 6:16, TLB).

No, a man's temptation is due to the pull of his own inward desires, which greatly attract him. It is his own desire which conceives and gives birth to sin (James 1: 14-15, J.B. Phillips).

Yielding to such desires (e.g., lust, anger, stealing, lying) allows the enemy to infiltrate our body, thus giving him control in whatever area we yielded to him. We are then in bondage to that spirit, and only Christ through the power of the Holy Spirit can evict that spirit, if we desire such to happen.

This is why in Ephesians 4:27 it says, *"Neither give place to the devil." Neither* is a continued negation of the previous verses telling us not to lie, not to be angry, etc., and *giving place* means giving a spot, room, opportunity, locality to the devil. We find examples in the Bible of spirits having a place in the lives of individuals.

One story, in particular, is seen in Matthew and Luke:

For if the demon leaves, it goes into the deserts [literally, passes through waterless places] for a while, seeking rest but finding none. Then it says, 'I will return to the man I came from.' So it returns and finds the man's heart clean but empty! Then the demon finds seven other spirits more evil than itself, and all enter the man and live in him, and so he is worse off than before (Matthew 12:43-45, TLB).

When a demon is cast out of a man, it goes to the deserts, searching there for rest, but finding none, it returns to the person it left, and finds that its former home is all swept and clean. Then it goes and gets seven other demons more evil than itself, and they all enter the man. And so the poor fellow is seven times (implied) worse off than he was before (Luke 11:24, TLB).

We read in Matthew 17:15 and 18,

Lord, have mercy on my son: for he is lunatick [mentally deranged], and sore vexed [in great trouble]: for ofttimes he falleth into the fire, and oft into the water...And Jesus rebuked the devil; and he departed out of him: and the child was cured from that very hour.

The father does not say it is a devil. He came to Jesus to get help for his son. Jesus rebuked the demon, establishing the fact that this sickness was caused by a spirit in the boy's life.

Once we understand and believe the truth— that there is a spirit world and that we do not battle flesh and blood but wrestle (figuratively, of the spiritual conflict engaged in by believers) —against such powers, we look at everything in a completely different light.

Many have a difficult time believing there are spirits of inheritance. Allow me to share God's word on the subject.

And when I punish people for their sins, the punishment continues upon the children, grandchildren, and great-grandchildren of those who hate me; but I lavish my love upon thousands of those who love me and obey my commandments (Exodus 20: 5-6, TLB).

Forgive us, even though you have said that you don't let sin go unpunished, and that you punish the father's fault in the children to the third and fourth generation (Numbers 14:18, TLB).

You shall not bow down to any images nor worship them in any way, for I am the Lord your God, I am a jealous God and I will bring the curse of a father's sins upon even the third and fourth generation of the children of those who hate me (Deuteronomy 5:9, TLB).

Many of us refuse to acknowledge that we have issues. We prefer to live in self-denial and be like the Pharisee—proud and self-righteous.

God, I thank thee, that I am not as other men [like everyone else]...for I never cheat, I don't commit adultery, I go without food twice a week, and I give to God a tenth of everything I earn." It would be much better to say, "God be merciful to me a sinner [literally, one who misses the mark] (Luke 18:11, TLB).

Once we accept that Satan has infiltrated our lives, it is much easier to understand the "mystery of iniquity" all around us. This is why in Luke 6:45 we read, *"A good man produces good deeds from a good heart and an evil man produces evil deeds from his hidden wickedness. Whatever is in the heart overflows into speech"* (TLB).

This kingdom of darkness inside of us must go! This brings us to the circle with the dove *(see Figure 5).* This circle represents God's kingdom in us.

First, the word *kingdom* means sovereignty, royal power, dominion, denoting the territory or people over whom a king rules. God's rule within believers is a mystery, implying knowledge withheld.

We know how Satan infiltrated our lives. How then does God place His kingdom (rule) in us?

Once we believe all have sinned, all fall short of God's glorious ideal, and repent—change your views and purpose to accept the will of God in your inner selves instead of rejecting it...And, as an expression of it, let everyone of you be baptized in the Name of Jesus Christ that you may have your sins forgiven [remission; to send away], then you also shall receive the gift of the Holy Spirit" (Romans 3:23, TLB).

It was John the Baptist who said in Matthew 3:11,

I indeed baptize you with water unto repentance: but he that cometh after me is mightier than I, whose shoes I am not worthy to bear: he shall baptize you with the Holy Ghost, and with fire.

In Matthew 4:23 we read

And Jesus went about all Galilee, teaching in their synagogues, and preaching the gospel [good news] of the kingdom, and healing all manner of sickness and all manner of disease among the people.

We are told in Romans 14:17, "For [assigning a reason, used in argument; explanation] *the kingdom* [realm; rule] *of God is not meat and drink; but righteousness, and peace, and joy in* [rest in a fixed position] *the Holy Ghost.* First Corinthians 4:20 says, *"For the kingdom of God is not in word, but in power."* This is why Jesus spoke to His apostles in Acts chapter 1 and commanded them to wait for the promise of the Father and be baptized with the Holy Ghost.

When this event took place, they were all filled with the Holy Ghost and began to speak with other tongues as the Spirit gave them utterance. They had now received a Kingdom within! God's Holy Spirit had come to them. *"Even the Spirit of truth; whom the world cannot receive, because it seeth him not, neither knoweth him: but ye know him; for he dwelleth with you, and shall be in you"* (John 14:17).

> *Wherefore we receiving [associate with oneself, in any familiar or intimate act or relation] a kingdom which cannot be moved, let us have grace [the divine influence upon the heart and its reflection in the life], whereby we may serve God acceptably [well pleasing] with reverence and godly fear* (Hebrews 12:28).

Once we receive His Holy Spirit, we are to be careful. We must consider all circumstances and possible consequences to help us govern and discipline our lives. We must rely upon the Holy Spirit in us to lead and guide us in all situations.

We read in Luke 17: 20-21,

> *The kingdom of God cometh not with observation [ocular evidence]: Neither shall they say, Lo here! or, lo there! for,*

behold, the kingdom of God is within [inside; denoting a fixed position in place, time or state] you.

We have within us two Kingdoms!
Satan's power and God's power!

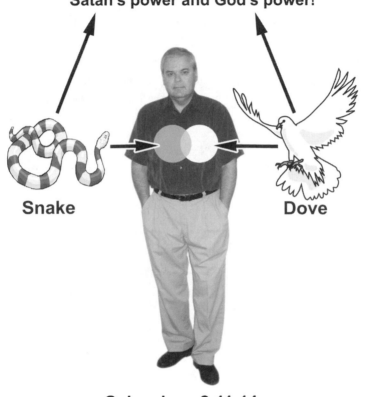

Snake **Dove**

Colossians 2:11-14
Romans 2:29
2 Corinthians 3:8-9
Phillipians 2:12-16

(Figure 5)

It is at this time God begins to work in us through His Spirit. He allows situations to develop to cause a reaction in us. Whatever, whoever He uses as a catalyst in any situation we find ourselves in, the purpose is to bring to the surface those entities the enemy has sown in our heart. This is why we are told *"And we know that all that happens to us is working for our good, if we love God and are fitting into His plans"* (Romans 8:28, TLB).

Once we believe in Jesus Christ as our personal Saviour, we then come to the realization that righteousness is a requirement in our lives. This can only be accomplished through the Holy Spirit. We know Abraham had faith for (with a view to) righteousness before he was circumcised. Faith brings the soul into vital union with God, and the Holy Spirit inevitably produces righteousness of life, that is, conformity to the will of God, as we submit to the lordship of Christ.

> *In whom also ye are circumcised with the circumcision made without hands, in putting off the body of the sins of the flesh by the circumcision of Christ* (Colossians 2:11).

"For he hath made him to be sin for us, who knew no sin; that we might be made [come into being] *the righteousness* [equity of character or act] *of God in him"* (2 Corinthians 5:21).

Deliverance through the Holy Spirit comes to us as we "renounce" (disown) the "hidden things" (concealed by covering, private, inward, keep secret) of "dishonesty" (shame or disgrace for oneself). We must be willing to respond when we are prayed for, by naming and casting away whatever it is that hinders our development as a believer.

Circumcision is to cut around! Spiritual circumcision of the heart and affections is the putting off the body of the sins of the flesh— Satan's kingdom in us. We do not have to live with lust, anger, rage, incest, etc. We can be free of the weights and sin that so easily beset us. Remember, we are not talking about a natural circumcision but a spiritual circumcision, effected by the Holy Spirit—God's kingdom within us. *"And circumcision is that of the heart, in the spirit, and not in the letter"* (Romans 2:29).

Once we understand that we can be liberated, delivered from those things in our lives that trouble us, we are then on our way to life in all its fullness (superior in quality).

Remember the story in Matthew 12:43-45 and Luke 11:24-26 where the unclean spirit is cast out of the man? Eventually, the unclean spirit returns to the house it was cast out of. It finds the man's house empty, swept, garnished. There is extremely important information that we must understand! Let us look at three words: *empty, swept, garnished* (from *The Complete*

Word Study New Testament with Greek Parallel).

Empty (4980) *schōlazō*: to take a holiday, i.e. be at leisure [by implication, devote oneself wholly to] a withholding of oneself from work, a vacation from employment

Swept (4563) *saroō*: to brush off; mean a broom; to sweep

Garnished (2885) *kōsmëō*: to put in proper order, i.e. decorate worldly

Note that the unclean spirit that was cast out of the man comes back and finds the individual has not filled his life with spiritual things, only worldly things. This, of course, gives the demon (spirit) opportunity to return with seven others to the house he was cast out from. This should not surprise us at all!

We are warned by the Lord in 1 John 2:15-17 with these words:

> *Stop loving this evil world and all that it offers you, for when you love these things you show that you do not really love God; For all these worldly things, these evil desires—the craze of sex, the ambition to buy everything that appeals to you, and the pride that comes from wealth and importance—these are not from God. They are from this evil world itself. And this world is fading away, and these evil, forbidden things will go*

*with it, but whoever keeps doing the will
of God will live forever"* (TLB).

The man in Matthew 12 and Luke 11 forgot
or disregarded this lesson and ended up in
major trouble again!

*Be careful—watch out for attacks from
Satan, your great enemy. He prowls
around like a hungry, roaring lion,
looking for some victim to tear apart"*
(1 Peter 5: 8, TLB).

It was Paul the Apostle who said, *"I'm not just
shadow-boxing or playing around"* (1
Corinthians 9:26, TLB).

We are in spiritual warfare!

We remind you again...

This Is a War!
Know Your Enemy!

We must not be ignorant of Satan's devices
(thoughts, that which is thought out). We must
trust in the Lord and lean (rely) not on our own
understanding (see Proverbs 3:5-6).

I remember praying for an individual who
had a very good witness before others as a
Christian. He had a wonderful wife and fine,
upstanding children. Through a series of
events, plotted by the devil, this man committed
adultery, shamed his family, disgraced himself
and almost committed murder! Only through

God's wonderful love and grace was this man restored. He was wonderfully delivered and is doing well today.

You and I cannot argue and/or have a conversation with the devil! He will and can out-think and out-talk us at every turn. Eve in the Garden of Eden tried and lost. Jesus answered the devil with God's Word through the Spirit!

It was Jesus who said,

> *Ye are of your father the devil, and the lusts of your father ye will do. He was a murderer from the beginning, and abode not in the truth, because there is no truth in him. When he speaketh a lie, he speaketh of his own; for he is a liar, and the father of it* (John 8:44).

The Living Bible paraphrases John 8:44 this way:

> *For you are the children of your father the devil and you love to do the evil things he does. He was a murderer from the beginning and a hater of truth— there is not an iota of truth in him. When he lies, it is perfectly normal; for he is the father of liars.*

I believe the Lord is coming again! I know when I say this there are some who laugh and scoff and continue to walk after their own lusts. They, no doubt, say that all things continue as they were—nothing has changed. In fact, in reality we know things are much worse, and perilous times are here.

We also believe God is not slack (slow) concerning His promise of coming again. He is long-suffering (that quality of self-restraint in the case of provocation, which does not hastily retaliate or promptly punish), not willing that any of us should perish (see 2 Peter 3:9).

God Wants to Show Us Mercy!

God has given to us, through His Son Jesus Christ, the tools to become "Righteous." We read: *"No one is good—no one in all the world is innocent"* (Romans 3:10, TLB). *"But no, all have strayed away; all are rotten with sin. Not one is good, not one"* (Psalm 14:3, TLB). *"We are all infected and impure with sin. When we put on our prized robes of righteousness, we find they are but filthy rags"* (Isaiah 64:6, TLB).

Our day is not much different than in the days of the Old Testament patriarch Noah. We read that in Noah's day man was morally very bad; the earth was corrupt and filled with violence (wrong). Every imagination (a thing framed, a plot of the thoughts) was evil continually. The reason was that Satan, the God of this world, had blinded (through self-conceit, pride, high-mindedness) their minds (the disbelieving), lest they should turn to God for the help they needed (see 2 Corinthians 4:4). Noah was a preacher of righteousness, and all the time he preached, he was building an ark. He realized judgment was coming, and he was told to prepare a way of escape. We know 120 years went by, and then came the flood. God's promised judgment came just as Noah had said, thus fulfilling God's word. Today, the whole world is under the influence of the evil one, Satan's *Invisible Government*!

God has not left us without a witness. We have His Word, the road map, the blueprint, if you will, of what we need to do and how to do it! We are without excuse!

Deliverance from demon power has been pooh-poohed by many, yet it is an answer to many of the issues we face as God's children. The Lord wants us clean inside, and He has given to us His power to achieve what, to many, seems impossible!

> *I am the true vine, and my Father is the husbandman. Every branch in me that beareth not fruit he taketh away: and every branch that beareth fruit, he pur-geth [cleanseth] it, that it may bring forth more fruit* (John 15:1-3).

We are, as the word says, to *abide* (stay) in Him and through Him, we are to bring forth much fruit.

We are told that,

> *If after they have escaped the pollutions [miasma; moral foulness; the effect:*

sully, taint] of the world through the knowledge [full discernment; fully acquainted with] of the Lord and Saviour Jesus Christ, they are again [once more] entangled [involved] therein, and overcome [vanquished], the latter end is worse with them than the beginning (2 Peter 2:20).

Remember,

When a demon is cast out of a man, it goes to the deserts, searching there for rest, but finding none, it returns to the person it left, and finds that its former home is all swept and clean. Then it goes and gets seven other demons more evil than itself, and they all enter the man and so the poor fellow is seven times [implied] worse off than he was before (Luke 11:24, TLB).

I have heard, many times, the saying, "The Holy Spirit cannot; will not; coexist with a demon!" This is very true. We are told that we are the temple of God, and the Spirit of God dwelleth in us (see 1 Corinthians 3:16). We must become aware, through the Holy Spirit in us, of those things within us—such as lying, anger, wrath, lust, etc.—that God wants cleansed. His power in us is sufficient to bring cleansing and set us free!

Remember, *"Out of the same mouth proceedeth blessing and cursing. My brethren, these things ought not so to be"* (James 3:10). *"Who is a wise man and endued with knowl-edge* [understanding] *among you? Let him shew out of a good conversation* [behaviour; manner of life] *his works with meekness of wisdom"* (James 3:13). If deliverance is true, and works in reality, then we should see the difference in those who profess to believe and say they have received it.

We are told to

> *Lay apart [put away; cast off] all filthi-ness [moral defilement] and superfluity [overflowing] of naughtiness [wicked-ness], and receive with meekness the engrafted [implanted] word, which is able to save [deliver or protect; make whole] your souls* (James 1:21).

> *We are told to "Confess [acknowledge] your faults [side-slip; lapse or deviation; unintentional error or willful transgres-sion, sin] one to another, and pray one for another, that ye may be healed [to cure; make whole]* (James 5:16).

Possibly the word *healed* in this verse includes both physical and spiritual healing.

Deliverance will help us to awake to righ-teousness and sin not. We too are building an ark. The ark we are building is within us. A change, transformation, is being effected—or should be—in us into the image of Christ by the

Holy Spirit! This change finds expression in our character and conduct.

> *Work [to finish, fashion, as a task] out your own salvation [deliverance; preservation], with fear and trembling. For it is God which worketh [to be active] in you both to will and to do of his good pleasure* (Philippians 2:12-13).

Remember! A tree is known (to know absolutely) by its fruit! Satan through his *Invisible Government* will try to stop this process through false doctrine, traditions, persecution, tribulation, cares of this world and the deceitfulness of riches. Being changed into the image of Christ is not what Satan wants for any of us!

This "mystery of Christ" in us was hid from ages and from generations. It has now been made manifest to us.

> *To whom God would make known what is the riches [fullness] of the glory of this mystery among the Gentiles; which is Christ in you, the hope of glory* (Colossians 1:27).

It was Paul the Apostle who said he preached, warned and taught every man so as to present every man perfect (complete—in labour, growth, mental and moral character) in Christ Jesus (see Colossians 1:28).

There are individuals who want all that God has for them. Like Abraham, they allow God to lead them, and they obey and honour His Word in order to grow spiritually. There are others, like Lot, who choose for themselves and are stunted in their spiritual growth. They do not consider all circumstances or possible consequences!

We must prepare now!

It was Paul who said,

> But we are bound to give thanks alway to God for you, brethren beloved of the Lord, because God hath from the beginning chosen [to take for oneself] you to salvation [rescue or safety] through sanctification [purification; to make holy] of the Spirit and belief of the truth: Whereunto [indicating the point reached or entered, of place, time or purpose] he called you by our gospel, to the obtaining [acquisition; the act or the thing; to make around oneself; acquire] of the glory of our Lord Jesus Christ (2 Thessalonians 2:13-14).

We are to take the advice given and prepare our ark. Noah built an ark with external equipment. We are to build our ark with internal equipment, notably, through His Holy Spirit!

- *What is it that hinders you in your walk with God?*

- *What is it that troubles you and causes you to go into depression or guilt?*

- *What is it that causes you to want to give up?*

> *Since we have such a huge crowd of men of faith watching us from the grandstands, let us strip off anything that slows us down or holds us back, and especially those sins that wrap themselves so tightly around our feet and trip us up; and let us run with patience the particular race that God has set before us"* (Hebrews 12:1, TLB).

We must demolish all reasoning, thoughts and every barrier that raises itself in opposition to the knowing of God. We must make prisoners of war every device and purpose and submit and obey the authority of Christ (see 2 Corinthians 10:5). The day is coming when those who have allowed the Holy Spirit to work within will be revealed! There are many today who have an appearance (semblance, formula) of piousness but contradict (disavow) the power (dunamis) of God. We are *"not ashamed of the gospel of Christ: for it is the power of God unto salvation* [rescue, or safety; physical or moral health; a deliverer] *to every one that believeth; to the Jew first, and also to the Greek* (Romans 1:16). As we have already stated, Noah prepared an ark, and when the flood came, Noah entered the ark and the Lord shut the door. We know Noah and his family were saved while others perished in the flood.

As we allow God's Holy Spirit to work within us, we read:

> *And the very God of peace sanctify [purify] you wholly [complete]; and I pray God your whole spirit and soul and body be preserved [to guard from loss or injury] blameless [faultless; irreproachable] unto [indicating the point reached or entered] the coming [a being near] of our Lord Jesus* (1 Thessalonians 5:23).

"For what is our hope, or joy, or crown of rejoicing? Are not even ye in the presence of our Lord Jesus Christ at his coming?" (1 Thessalonians 2:19). Remember these words: *"Follow peace with all men, and holiness, without which no man shall see* [gaze with wide-open eyes at something remarkable] *the Lord"* (Hebrews 12:14).

We are told to *"Watch therefore: for ye know not what hour your Lord doth come...Therefore be ye also ready* [fitness; adjusted; made ready]: *for in such an hour as ye think not the Son of man cometh"* (Matthew 24:42-44).

"No man, having put his hand to the plough, and looking back [voluntary observation], *is fit* [well placed; appropriate for] *the kingdom of God"* (Luke 9:62). There are some, like Lot in the Old Testament, who will settle for less in the spiritual if they can enjoy and indulge their desires in the natural—this present world. We read how, after God judged Sodom and Gomorrah, Lot entered a place called Zoar (little, to be small, ignoble, be brought low) (see Genesis 19). His was a lesser place spiritually. He, as we know, lost some of his family due to the way he conducted his life spiritually. He "vexed" (tortured) his righteous soul in "voluntary observation" and hearing (the act, the sense or the thing heard) with the "filthy conversation" (behaviour) of the wicked! We are told to be holy as He (God) is holy (1 Peter 1:15-16)! *"His divine power hath given unto us all things that pertain unto life and godliness"* (2 Peter 1:3); yet some would tell us it is not necessary to receive deliverance. Everything is fine, and, of course, if or when we sin, we have forgiveness through Jesus Christ! They will quote *"And if any man sin, we have an* advocate [an intercessor, comforter (*Parousia*] *with the Father, Jesus Christ the righteous"* (1 John 2:1).

Let us look at the first part of 1 John 2:1: *"My little children, these things write I unto you, **that ye sin not**. And **if** any man sin..."* (emphasis added). In other words, if something happens and we sin, God can and will forgive us. Look around you without the "rose-coloured" glasses and face the stark reality of what we see in our churches. It is not a pretty sight and is an indictment on those who profess to be Christians. Whether we agree or not, the world is not blind to what it sees in the churches and judges us accordingly!

The inhabitants of Sodom judged Lot by his behaviour, and when the time came to warn the people concerning God's judgment to come, they only laughed at him in total disbelief. The old saying "What you are speaks so loud, I cannot hear what you are saying" is very true!

Let us look at what happens in us and what will happen to us as we submit to God's cleansing within. He will increase (to grow, enlarge) and we will decrease (lessen in rank or influence) (see John 3:30). We are told,

> Let no man despise [to think against, disesteem] thy youth; but be thou an example [Tüpos] type; model of some reality that was yet to appear; a proto-type or that which was yet to be developed and evolved; style, resemblance] of the believers, in word, in conversation [behaviour], in charity [love], in spirit, in faith, in purity [cleanliness; chastity; moral attitude] (1 Timothy 4:12).

It is important that we live our life now in the light of eternity! Once we realize and understand that God has a plan for our lives, then it is our responsibility, with God's help, to accomplish and fulfill His will for us and in us.

One person in the Bible who stands out as one who minimized God's will for his life is Esau. He sold his birthright for bread and a pottage of lentils. He lost the blessing that went with his birthright. In Hebrews 12:16 we read,

> *Lest there be any fornicator, or profane person, as Esau, who for one morsel of meat [food] sold his birthright." The Living Bible paraphrases it as follows: Watch out that no one becomes involved in sexual sin or becomes careless about God as Esau did. He traded his rights as the oldest son for a single meal.*

Another right was that of the double portion. Connected with the birthright was the progenitorship (an ancestor in the direct line; a forefather) of the Messiah. Esau despised his spiritual privilege. Hebrews 2:1 says, *"So we must listen carefully to the truths we have heard, or we may drift away from them"* (TLB).

It is the job of the enemy (Satan) to destroy, if possible, what God has planned for the human race. Satan's *Invisible Government* is constantly at work with his schemes; yet we know and are not ignorant of his devices—or should not be.

God desires to bring us back to the glory that was lost because of sin!

Man is not what God intended him to be!

He lacks God's image and character!

"For all have sinned, and come short [to be inferior, be deficient, be in want] *of the glory of God"* (Romans 3:23). *"And the glory which thou gavest me I have given them; that they may be one, even as we are one"* (John 17:22). What does the word *glory* mean in these verses? Primarily, it signifies an opinion, estimate, and hence, the honour resulting from a good opinion. It would denote the manifested perfection of Christ's character, especially His righteousness—of which we all fall short! God, through Christ, wants to exhibit in and through us His character and righteousness! How is this done?

In 2 Corinthians 3:18 we read,

> *But we Christians have no veil over our faces; we can be mirrors that brightly reflect the glory of the Lord. And as the Spirit of the Lord works within us, we become more and more like Him* (TLB).

Satan has done a wonderful job of concealing the truth about deliverance. He has joined the college of theologians and has mass-produced his doctrinal lies to avoid detection. He has divided God's people into religious factions, knowing that a house divided against itself cannot stand (see Mark 3:25). Through false teaching, he has hindered many from receiving the baptism in the Holy Spirit. Through false teaching, he has promoted the idea that Christians, believers, cannot have a demon (spirit). Through his lies, he has hidden his evil spirits in the lives of many and then through another lie suggests the issues, problems, we have are the works of the flesh. What a liar he is, and the sad part of it all is that many believe him. Behind every work is an entity, a real being or species of being—in this case, an evil spirit. I am not denying that we have a fallen nature! I am also not denying that we have a sin principle (meaning that from which anything proceeds; a source or origin; a primordial substance) existing from the beginning.

> *Happy is the man who doesn't give in and do wrong when he is tempted, for afterwards he will get as his reward the crown of life that God has promised those who love him. And remember, when someone wants to do wrong, it is never God who is tempting him, for God never wants to do wrong and never tempts anyone else to do it. Temptation is the pull of man's own evil thoughts and wishes. These evil thoughts lead to evil actions and afterwards, to the death*

penalty from God. So don't be misled, dear brothers (James 1:12-16, TLB).

Satan has tried through the centuries to destroy God's plan of having fellowship with man. He has not and will not succeed, even though it looks at times that he has or will! God is working in believers who have allowed the Holy Spirit to lead them to the truths in God's Word to bring victory to their Christian walk!

Let us stop going over the same old ground again and again, always teaching those first lessons about Christ. Let us go on instead to other things and become mature in our understanding, as strong Christians ought to be. Surely we don't need to speak further about the foolishness of trying to be saved by being good, or about the necessity of faith in God; you don't need further instruction about baptism and spiritual gifts and the resurrection of the dead and eternal judgment. The Lord willing, we will go on now to other things (Hebrews 6:1-3, TLB).

Once we have accepted and received deliverance, depending on our individual issues (inward battles), the question arises as to how we retain the ground we have regained from the enemy. For the answer to this question, we must look at the provision the Lord has given to us.

The Lord has told us that He will provide, and you will see how true this is as we look at the armour of light.

The night is far gone; the day of His return will soon be here. So quit the evil deeds of darkness and put on the "Armor of Right Living," as we who live in the daylight should! Be decent and true in everything you do so that all can approve your behavior. Don't spend your time in wild parties and getting drunk or in adultery and lust, or fighting or jealousy. But ask the Lord Jesus Christ to help you live as you should, and don't make plans to enjoy evil" (Romans 13:12-14, TLB).

We read about the armour of light in Ephesians 6:10-19.

"Last of all I want to remind you that your strength must come from the Lord's mighty power within you. Put on all of God's armor so that you will be able to stand safe against all strategies and tricks of Satan" (Ephesians 6:10-11, TLB).

Remember—the battle is not yours, but God's!

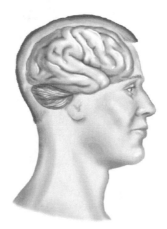

(Figure 6)

We know the mind is the battleground on which Satan wages war. "Put on all of God's armor so that you will be able to stand safe against all strategies and tricks of Satan...But to do this you will need the strong belt of truth" (Ephesians 6:10-14, TLB). "Wherefore gird up the loins of your mind" (1 Peter 1:13).

"Loins of your mind" is used metaphorically. The mind, as we know, is "deep thought; the faculty; its exercise or understanding; perception." Your mental powers alert to the reality clearly lying before our eyes, as opposed to mere appearance without reality. For example, *"Is it lawful to give tribute to Caesar, or not?...But he, knowing their hypocrisy, said unto them, Why tempt ye me?* (Mark 12:14-15).

The Holy Spirit is our beam of balance or yoke. He is our coupling to the truth—reality. He will enable us to know the truth, as opposed to falsehood, error or insincerity. We do not want to be outsmarted by Satan. We must always be on our guard against the trickery of Satan!

I recall a situation when I prayed with a girl who had a lesbian spirit. This spirit had penetrated her life when she was a teenager. Her mother was not married at the time she gave birth, and after some time had elapsed, the mother married someone else. As the girl grew up, her stepfather would not permit her to date young men, fearing she would do what her mother had done. The girl would then go to her room and fantasize that she was a boy going out with girls. The fantasizing eventually became reality, and when she wanted to go out, she would tell her stepfather she was going out with her girlfriend. Eventually a spirit of lesbianism entered her life, and in reality she became the male figure in her relationships with girls. Through a series of events, God in His great love and mercy set this girl free from this perverted spirit. Today she lives in victory and is totally free. Such a change can only be effected through becoming a believer in Jesus Christ and receiving His power, enabling us to live victoriously.

We are told:

It is true that I am an ordinary, weak human being, but I don't use human plans and methods to win my battles. I use God's mighty weapons, not those made by men, to knock down the devil's strongholds. These weapons can break down every proud argument against God and every wall that can be built to keep men from finding Him" (2 Corinthians 10:3-5, TLB).

This is why we are told to *"Be careful* [to be anxious about; through the idea of distraction] *for nothing; but in every thing by prayer* [request; involves the idea of urgent need] *and supplication with thanksgiving* [grateful language to God] *let your requests* [asking] *be made known unto God* (Philippians 4:6). Peace, rest and quietness will come to your emotions. Your heart and mind will be protected through the Lord Jesus Christ. You might ask, "Will I still have other thoughts come to my mind"? Yes! Other thoughts (negative) will battle for supremacy.

There is a wonderful prescription given to us in Philippians 4:4-8:

Delight yourselves in God, yes, find your joy in Him at all times. Have a reputation for gentleness, and never forget the nearness of your Lord. Don't worry over anything whatever; tell God every detail of your needs in earnest and thankful prayer, and the peace of God, which transcends human understanding, will keep constant guard over your hearts and minds as they rest in Christ Jesus" (TLB).

Here is a last piece of advice:

If you believe in goodness and if you value the approval of God, fix your minds on whatever is true and honourable and just and pure and lovely and admirable (Philippians 4:8, J.B. Phillips).

You might say, "I can't do this; no one can!" We read, *"I can do all things through Christ which strengtheneth me"*(Philippians 4:13). *"For I can do everything God asks me to with the help of Christ who gives me the strength and power"* (TLB).

Knowing we can do all things through Christ, we can discipline ourselves to think on the things that are positive and acceptable (see Philippians 4:8), therefore gaining the victory in our minds. Trusting in Him will bring a rest (peace) in your life. You will stop trying and begin trusting! We have already shown that we are not fighting against people made of flesh and blood. We are fighting an evil spirit world (an unseen world)! Because of this, we must use every piece of God's armour to resist the enemy whenever he attacks and still be standing when the attack is over.

We are to "stand fast" (see Galatians 5:1). We are to "resist" (oppose) the devil (see James 4:7), knowing we have truth on our side—the Word of God as the weapon to stop all doubt, confusion and lies the enemy uses to penetrate our armor! The breastplate of faith and love will protect against the enemy's fiery darts. If we have faith and love in our Lord Jesus Christ and also toward our fellowman, nothing will be able to penetrate inwardly. Bitterness, envy, jealousy, hate, anger, etc., are those issues that hurt us inwardly. We must realize and learn (in any way)—whatever the condition or state in which we exist—to be content, thus raising a barrier and warding off the enemy.

How many times have we allowed ourselves to be drawn away from our abiding in Him, only to be trapped by the enemy in scenarios that only hurt us? We must rely totally on the Holy Spirit within us! He will lead and teach us and, at times, will speak to us in such a direct manner that we will know without a doubt what we must do!

The Breastplate of Righteousness

"And *having on the breastplate of righteous-ness*" (Ephesians 6:14). This breastplate consisted of two parts, protecting the body on both sides, from the neck to the middle. We know that God wants to produce His righteousness in us through the Holy Spirit. Conformity to the revealed will of God through voluntary submission to the control of the Holy Spirit is what God requires from us. *"Putting on the breastplate of faith and love"* (1 Thessalonians 5:8).

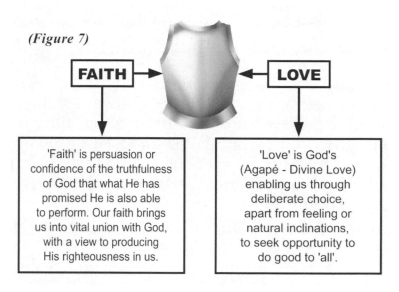

(Figure 7)

FAITH		LOVE
'Faith' is persuasion or confidence of the truthfulness of God that what He has promised He is also able to perform. Our faith brings us into vital union with God, with a view to producing His righteousness in us.		'Love' is God's (Agapé - Divine Love) enabling us through deliberate choice, apart from feeling or natural inclinations, to seek opportunity to do good to 'all'.

The breastplate, then, is a metaphor for faith and love, thus preventing the enemy from hindering our growth in God. Remember, it is God who is working within us (Philippians 2:13)! We must "work out" (Philippians 2:12)—perform—what God is working within, as obedient children. It is willing subjection to that which we know as the revealed will of God.

We have many examples of this in the Bible. *"Then the Spirit said unto Philip"* (Acts 8:29). *"And the Lord said unto him..."* (Acts 9:11). *"While Peter thought on the vision, the Spirit said* unto him..." (Acts 10:19). *And the Spirit bade me go with them..."* (Acts 11:12). *"The Holy Ghost said..."* (Acts 13:2). *"And were forbidden of the Holy Ghost..."* (Acts 16:6).

This can and will take place in our Christian walk! Once we understand and allow deliverance to work within us, internal fitness will come as the result of cleansing. It will be much easier to trust and surrender to the Holy Spirit and give Him the control He desires in our lives. In other words, surrender to Him, and your Christian walk will become a joy, and abundant living will be yours.

I have learned to be content in whatsoever state (circumstances) I find myself in (see Philippians 4:11). It was Paul who said,

> *I am crucified with Christ: nevertheless I live; yet not I, but Christ liveth in me: and the life which I now live in the flesh I live by the faith of the Son of God, who loved me, and gave himself for me* (Galatians 2:20).

Let us now look at the piece of armour that, to me, brings everything we have said into perspective.

The Helmet of Salvation

"And take the helmet of salvation..."
(Ephesians 6:17).

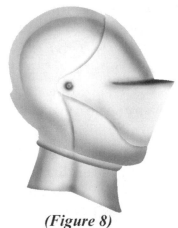

(Figure 8)

What does this mean? The answer is found in 1 Thessalonians 5:8: *"and for an helmet, the hope of salvation."* We are told the "helmet" (encirclement of the head) is the "hope" (to anticipate, usually with pleasure; expectation or confidence) of salvation (rescue or safety). Further investigation takes us to Colossians 1:26-27:

> *Even the mystery which hath been hid from ages and from generations, but now is made manifest to his saints: To whom God would make known what is the riches of the glory of this mystery among the Gentiles; which is Christ in you, the hope of glory (emphasis added).*

We have already stated that the day of Christ is coming, and when that day comes, it will reveal those who have submitted to the rule of

Christ within them—those who have allowed His Holy Spirit to work and to do of His good pleasure (Philippians 2:13).

This is why in Romans 8:18 we read: "For I reckon that the sufferings of this present time are not worthy to be compared **with the glory which shall be revealed in us** (emphasis added).

> *For it became him, for whom are all things, and by whom are all things, in bringing [leading] many sons unto [indicating the point reached or entered] glory, to make the captain [author] of their salvation perfect [complete] through sufferings. For both he that sanctifieth [purify; make holy] and they who are sanctified [purified; made holy] are all of one: for which cause [logical reason] he is not ashamed to call them brethren* (Hebrews 2:10-11).

It is no wonder that we are told "*And every man that hath this hope in him purifieth* [to make clean] *himself, even as he is pure* (1 John 3:3). Like Noah, we are making preparation—in this case, internal fitness within. We are holding the "mystery" of the faith in a pure conscience!

> *But seek ye first [in time, place, order or importance] the kingdom of God, and his righteousness; and all these things shall be added unto you* (Matthew 6:33).

Our first priority is seeking God's righteousness through His Holy Spirit within us, We are told in this chapter that food, clothing, etc., will be provided. We are not to be anxious about these things; yet, I am sad to say, many are. There is an informative Scripture in 1 Corinthians 7:31:

> And they that use [furnish what is needed] this world, as not abusing [misusing; overusing] it: for the fashion [actions, manner of life] of this world passeth away.

God *will* supply our need(s), but we must seek above all else His character or all that He requires us to be. Conformity to the will of God through our obedience to His kingdom (rule) within should be the highest priority in our lives!

We know He is coming again.

> "Behold, I come as a thief. Blessed is he that watcheth [to keep awake, be vigilant], and keepeth [to guard from loss or injury] his [inner or outer] garments, lest he walk naked, and they see [simply voluntary observation] his shame [shapeless, inelegant]" (Revelation 16:15).

There are many who will receive a rude awakening. They were given the *earnest* (pledge; token of what is to come) of the Spirit to work out the change in character, conduct and moral conformity waiting for the hope of righteousness in Him (see Ephesians 1:14). Nothing will happen "in and to" them. We need to understand and know what the hope of His calling and what is the fullness of the glory of His inheritance in us. When we do, we will also realize He has given to us the power through His Holy Spirit to attain to this high calling (see Ephesians 1:18-19)!

> *Now Glory be to God who by His mighty power at work within us is able to do far more than we would ever dare to ask or even dream of—infinitely beyond our highest prayers, desires, thoughts or hopes* (Ephesians 3:20, TLB).

> *I am sure that God who began the good work within you will keep right on helping you grow in His grace until His task within you is finally finished on that day when Jesus Christ returns* (Philippians 1:6, TLB).

It was Paul the Apostle who said,

> *I therefore so run, not as uncertainly; so fight I, not as one that beateth the air: But I keep under my body, and bring it into subjection: lest that by any means, when I have preached to others, I myself should be a castaway [approved worthless]* (1 Corinthians 9:26-27).

Or, As the Living Bible paraphrases:

So I run straight to the goal with purpose in every step. I fight to win. I'm not just shadow boxing or playing around, like an athlete I punish my body, treating it roughly, training it to do what it should, not what it wants to. Otherwise I fear that after enlisting others for the race, I myself might be declared unfit and ordered to stand aside.

"And Jesus said unto him, No man, having put his hand to the plough, and looking back, is fit [well adapted, appropriate] *for the kingdom of God"* (Luke 9:62). God places His Kingdom within us!

Wherefore we receiving [(Paralambano) associate with oneself, in any familiar or intimate act or relation] a kingdom which cannot be moved [unshaken], let us have grace [the divine influence upon our hearts and its reflection in our lives], whereby we may serve God acceptably [fully agreeable] with reverence [awe] and godly fear [caution, carefully, i.e., circumspect; prudent; examining carefully all the circumstances that may affect a determination] (Hebrews 12:28).

It will take His Kingdom within to give us an entrance into the Kingdom of Heaven!

Second Peter 1:3 tells us,

> *According as his divine power hath given unto us all things that pertain unto life and godliness [does what is well pleasing to Him], through the knowledge [full discernment] of him that hath called us to glory and virtue [intrinsic excellence].*

Peter lists the qualities that should be in us to make us fruitful and not useless or barren. It is our responsibility to make our calling (divine) and selection sure (steadfast). We then shall have an entrance (indicating the point reached; progress) ministered unto us abundantly into the perpetual Kingdom (realm; rule) of our Lord and Saviour Jesus Christ!

This, of course, reminds me of the parable (to compare as a spiritual lesson) of the ten virgins. The five wise virgins were ready (adjusted; fitness) and entered with the bridegroom to the marriage. The others were left outside, as they were not ready. We must prepare now, not later! Once we understand deliverance and God's purpose for our lives, we will, with God's help, prepare ourselves for His coming.

There are three Greek words that I find extremely interesting relating to the coming of the Lord. They are *Parousia*, *Apokalupsis* and *Epiphaneia*. Let us look at these three words, what they could mean and how they might relate to you and me.

The definition of the word *Parousia*, according *to Strong's Greek Dictionary of the New Testament,* is "a being near, coming, being present." The word is used many times in Scripture, and I will quote two Scriptures to establish its meaning.

> *I am glad of the coming [Parousia] of Stephanas and Fortunatus and Achailus: for that which was lacking on your part they have supplied* (1 Corinthians 16:17).

Here we see Stephanas and others coming to be present or near Paul.

> *Nevertheless God, that comforteth those that are cast down, comforted us by the coming [Parousia] of Titus; And not by his coming [Parousia] only, but by the consolation wherewith he was comforted in you, when he told us your earnest desire, your mourning, your fervent mind toward me; so that I rejoiced the more* (2 Corinthians 7:6-7).

Here Titus came to be near Paul the Apostle. The definition of the word *Apokalupsis,* according *to Strong's Greek Dictionary of the New Testament,* is: "disclosure, manifestation, be revealed, to take off the cover, i.e., disclose." This word is also used many times in Scripture, and I will quote a few Scriptures to establish its meaning.

"For the earnest expectation of the creature waiteth for the manifestation [Apokalupsis] *of the sons of God"* (Romans 8:19).

Now to him that is of power to stablish you according to my gospel, and the preaching of Jesus Christ, according to the revelation [Apokalupsis] of the mystery, which was kept secret since the world began (Romans 16:25).

So that ye come behind [to be later; to be inferior] in no gift; waiting [to expect fully] for the coming [Apokalupsis] of our Lord Jesus Christ (1 Corinthians 1:7).

To reveal [Apokalupsis] his Son in me, that I might preach him among the heathen; immediately I conferred not with flesh and blood (Galatians 1:16).

But rejoice, inasmuch as ye are partakers of Christ's sufferings; that, when his glory shall be revealed [Apokalupsis], ye may be glad also with exceeding joy (1 Peter 4:13).

The definition of the word *Epiphaneia*, according to *Strong's Greek Dictionary of the New Testament*, is: a manifestation, appearing, brightness, to become visible, conspicuous, shining forth.

Looking [to await with confidence or patience] for that blessed hope, and the glorious appearing [Epiphaneia] of the great God and our Saviour Jesus Christ (Titus 2:13).

Looking forward to that wonderful time we've been expecting, when His Glory shall be seen—the Glory of our great God and Savior Jesus Christ (Titus 2:13, TLB).

I charge thee therefore before God, and the Lord Jesus Christ, who shall judge the quick and the dead at his appearing [Epiphaneia] and his kingdom (2 Timothy 4:1).

Remember when we said the Kingdom of God does not come with observation? *"The kingdom of God is within* [inside] *you"* (Luke 17:20-21). One day, His Kingdom "in you" will be visible! The Scripture that comes to mind is, *"But as many as received him, to them gave he power to become* [come into being] *the sons of God, even to them that believe on his name"* (John 1:12).

We realize that it is not apparent, yet, what we shall be, but we know that when Jesus Christ shows himself (or appears or is manifested), we shall be like (similar in appearance or character) Him! Why? Because we shall "See" (gaze with wide-open eyes, as at something remarkable) Him as He is (1 John 3:2). 1 John

3:3 says *"every man that hath this hope in him purifieth* [to make clean] *himself, even* [inasmuch] *as he is pure* [clean; perfect].

This is why we read in 1 John 2:28,

> *And now, little children, abide in him; that, when he shall appear [be manifested], we may have confidence [boldness], and not be ashamed [disgraced; disfigured] before him at his coming [Parousia].*

To "appear" could mean to be visible, to be obvious as a subject of observation. To be "manifested" is to be revealed in one's true character.

Deliverance might not be the "panacea" or remedy for everything we need as believers, but it is certainly part of the whole for victory in our Christian walk. Many of us have realized we have come to a spiritual plateau and cannot seem to go deeper in the Lord. If you know what is holding you back, there is a possibility that you might need deliverance!

Once the coming of His presence (*Parousia*) with His people happens, there will come an unveiling and uncovering (*Apokalupsis*), a shining forth (*Epiphaneia*) of the Glory of God from those who have prepared for such a day!

> *Now to him that is of power to stablish [make fast; fix] you according to my gospel, and the preaching of Jesus Christ, according to the revelation [dis-*

closure] of the mystery, which was kept secret since the world began (Romans 16:25).

God calls upon everyone everywhere, without distinction of race or nationality, to submit voluntarily to His rule within. We read, *"And [Jesus] was transfigured before them: and his face did shine as the sun, and his raiment was white as the light"* (Matthew 17:2).

And he [Jesus] said unto them, Verily I say unto you, That there be some of them that stand here, which shall not taste of death, till they have seen the kingdom of God come with power. And after six days Jesus taketh with him Peter, and James, and John, and leadeth them up into an high mountain apart by themselves: and he was transfigured [to transform, change; Mëtamorphōō] before them. And his raiment became shining [to gleam, i.e., flash intensely], exceeding white as snow; so as no fuller [a carding comb; a cloth carder or dresser] on earth can white them (Mark 9:1-3).

Here we see the miracle of transformation from an earthly form into a supernatural one. This process is already taking place within us as we allow the Holy Spirit to work within.

Remember, *"Neither shall they say, Lo here! or, lo there! for, behold, the kingdom of God is within you"* (Luke 17:21).

> *And be not conformed [to fashion, conform to] to this world [age]: but be ye transformed [invisible process in Christians that is taking place now] by the renewing [renovation] of your mind [perception; apprehension], that ye may prove [discern; approve] what is that good [intrinsic], and acceptable [fully agreeable], and perfect [complete, fully completed growth], will of God* (Romans 12:2).

What a remarkable thing to see, to gaze with wide-opened eyes at someone (in this case, Jesus) changing into a supernatural form! No wonder we are told,

> *And that servant, which knew [to know absolutely] his lord's will [purpose; gracious design], and prepared [internal fitness] not himself, neither did according to his will, shall be beaten with many stripes* (Luke 12:47, emphasis added).

We who are believers know that we are children of God. We also know we have been given the Holy Spirit to work within us to will and to do of His good pleasure (Philippians 2:13). Our submission to His rule (authority) in us will conform us into His image or fashion us like unto Him. No one knows when they look at you what is taking place inside your life. They looked at Jesus, and many never realized who He was or understood His message. The apostles Peter, James and John had a preview when He (Jesus) was transfigured before them. We are told, "*It doth not yet appear* [to render apparent] *what we shall be: but we know that, when he shall appear, we shall be like* [similar in appearance or character]. Think of this remarkable, miraculous happening! We are to be manifested in our true character! The question then comes to mind, whose character will be revealed or be evident, His or ours?

> *For we through the Spirit wait [to expect fully] for the hope [to anticipate, usually with pleasure or confidence] of righteousness [in character or act] by faith [persuasion, moral conviction of religious truth; belief]* (Galatians 5:5).

It was Paul the Apostle who said that some would agitate and corrupt or transmute the gospel of Christ. To him, the gospel of Christ meant disowning the concealed or private, hidden things of shame (to feel shame for oneself or disgrace) to allow the Glory of God to be revealed in and through him by the Holy Spirit. Paul was not ashamed of the gospel (good news) of Christ (Romans 1:16). He realized it was the power (*dunamis*: special miraculous power) of God given to change (transform: *metamorphose*) us into the same image (likeness, resemblance) of the Lord.

There are those who have an appearance of godliness but deny the working of God's power within (2 Timothy 3:5). We are told not to let sin reign in our mortal bodies, neither to yield our members as instruments of unrighteousness unto sin (Romans 6:12-13). We are to walk (activities of our life) in righteousness with the Holy Spirit's help.

We all know the fruit of the Spirit is the visible expression of power working inwardly and invisibly.

The Character of the Fruit Is Evidence of the Character of the Power Producing It!

We read, *"Ye shall know them by their fruits"* (Matthew 7:16) or *"You can detect them by the way they act, just as you can identify a tree by its fruit"* (TLB). If, as we believe, love, joy, peace, long-suffering, gentleness, goodness, faith, meekness and temperance are the fruit of the Holy Spirit, then adultery, fornication, uncleanness, etc., is the fruit of other spirits! Remember *"that to whom ye yield yourselves servants to obey, his servants ye are to whom ye obey* (Romans 6:16).

Sinful flesh or "flesh of sin" is organized power acting through the members of our bodies. This is why Cain in Genesis 4:7 was told, *"If thou doest well, shalt thou not be accepted? and if thou doest not well, sin lieth* [to crouch on all four legs, folded like a recumbent, idle, inactive animal] *at the door* [entranceway].

Remember this: the Character of the Fruit (Deed) Is Evidenced by the Power Producing It!

God has given to us, through the Holy Spirit, diversities of gifts (charisma), spiritual endowments (1 Corinthians 12:4). One of those endowments is "discerning of spirits" (1 Corinthians 12:10). Why? To break the bondages in our lives in order to serve the Lord with abundant lives and become servants of righteousness, having fruit unto (indicating the point reached or entered) holiness (purification, i.e., the state of purity). God is purifying (purging, cleansing) *"unto himself a peculiar* [special; one's own] *people, zealous of good works* (Titus 2:14).

We read in Hebrews 12:1,

> *Let us strip off everything that hinders us, as well as the sin which dogs our feet, and let us run the race that we have to run with patience, our eyes fixed on Jesus the source and the goal of our faith* (J.B. Phillips).

We can have a weight of grief, a weight of care, a weight of poverty, etc. These are impediments that hinder our spiritual progress, and they must be removed from our lives.

I prayed for a mother who had a spirit of grief. Her son died due to a severe stroke, and she could not get past the emotional pain it caused her. Sadness and depression became weights that needed to be cast off in order for her to move on in God.

We are told in Philippians 3:13, "*forgetting* [to lose out of mind] *those things which are behind*," or "I leave the past behind," yet there are some who cannot do this, and in many cases they need some deliverance from the spirit world.

I also prayed for a woman who, as a child, was placed with her mother in a concentration camp. For many years she carried as weights all the emotional pain and suffering she endured in that camp, until the Lord brought deliverance to her life. We must stop looking back with sorrowful longing at something done or left undone. We must run with cheerful (or hopeful) endurance the contest set before us (Hebrews 12:1). As we have stated previously, we are in a spiritual war with an *Invisible Government*. The kingdom of heaven must be possessed by those who are determined to receive the prize, not yielding to the opposition of the spirit world through whatever means it uses to fight against us.

My question to you as you read this book is, "Will you be ashamed at His appearing?"

- Ashamed because of indecorous (improper) conduct that has impaired your growth in the Lord Jesus Christ?

- Ashamed because you denied the inward working power of God given to you by your heavenly Father to change you into the image of His Son?

- *Ashamed:* To feel shame, degraded, disgraced by a consciousness of guilt resulting from neglect of the truth.

We read in Hebrews 2:1-3,

> *Therefore we ought to give the more earnest heed to the things which we have heard, lest at any time we should let them slip. For if the word spoken by angels was stedfast, and every transgression and disobedience received a just recompence of reward; How shall we escape, if we neglect so great salvation; which at the first began to be spoken by the Lord, and was confirmed unto us by them that heard him.*

> *So we must listen very carefully to the truths we have heard, or we may drift away from them. For since the messages from angels have always proved true and people have always been punished for disobeying them, what makes us think that we can escape if we are*

indifferent to this great salvation announced by the Lord Jesus himself, and passed on to us by those who heard Him speak?" (TLB).

PRAYER

Lord Jesus, I bow my heart in your presence, acknowledging to you my need of deliverance. I bring to you now those weights and sins that have troubled me for so long. I now know and believe that as I renounce them, the Holy Spirit will set me free. My complete desire is to have the character of Jesus Christ manifested through me at Your coming. I want to be diligent and found by You in peace, without spot and blameless.

Amen!

We would love to hear how God has touched your life through this book. Please feel free to contact us at revgeog@aol.com or visit our Web site @ http://www.areyoubound.com/.

Direct inquiries to:
Rev. G. LeRoy
34A Avondale Blvd.
P.O. Box 83075
Brampton, ON L6T 5N3

For Deliverance Ministry,
see Lake Hamilton Bible Camp at:
Telephone: (501) 525-8204
Hot Springs, Ark. 71913
E-mail: 72lhbc@cablelynx.com
Web site:
http://www.lakehamiltonbiblecamp.com/

GLOSSARY

But those things which proceed out of the mouth come forth from the heart; and they defile the man. For out of the heart proceed evil thoughts, murders, adulteries, fornications, thefts, false witness, blasphemies (Matthew 15:18-19).

Evil Thoughts: evil in effect, influence, internal considerations, purpose

Murders: infanticide (babies); matricide (mother); patricide (father)

Adulteries: having a paramour (a lover or a mistress who unlawfully takes the place of a husband or wife), a lover, a wooer; having sexual intercourse with someone other

	than their husband or wife
Fornications:	to have illicit sexual inter-course, said of unmarried persons; to indulge in unlawful lust; incest (sexual cohabitation with relatives)
Theft:	stealing (pilfering, filching)
False Witness:	untrue testimony; lying; habit of lying
Blasphemies:	vilification (defamation) against God; impious; evil speaking; slander

For from within, out of the heart of men, proceed evil thoughts, adulteries, forni-cations, murders, Thefts, covetousness, wickedness, deceit, lasciviousness, an evil eye, blasphemy, pride, foolishness: All these evil things come from within, and defile the man" (Mark 7:21-23).

Covetousness:	greed; desiring more; extortion; avarice; fraudulency
Wickedness:	malice; plots
Deceit:	delude; to decoy, allure
Lasciviousness:	no restraint; incontinent; filthy; licentious; loose
Evil Eye:	envy; jealous side glance
Pride:	haughty; appearing above others

Foolishness: senselessness; egotism; reck-lessness; folly; unwise; acting without discretion

Being filled with all unrighteousness, fornication, wickedness, covetousness, maliciousness; full of envy, murder, debate, deceit, malignity; whisperers, Backbiters, haters of God, despiteful, proud, boasters, inventors of evil things, disobedient to parents, Without under-standing, covenantbreakers, without natural affection, implacable, unmer-ciful: Who knowing the judgment of God, that they which commit such things are worthy of death, not only do the same, but have pleasure in them that do them (Romans 1:29-32).

Maliciousness: badness; naughtiness; spiteful; deliberate intention to injure

Debate: wrangling; contention; strife

Malignity: evil disposition of heart toward another; deep-rooted spite; ani-mosity; rancour (ill will)

Whisperer: to utter an untruth, deceive by falsehood; one who slanders secretly

Backbiter: talkative against; secret slander

Haters of God: impious

Despiteful: an insulter, maltreater; use despitefully, offend

Boaster: braggart; a vain person

Inventors of Evil Things:

discoverer, contriver, one who plans or devises (schemer) evil things

Disobedient to Parents:

unpersuadable; refusing to obey

Without Understanding:
unintelligent; wicked

Covenant Breakers:
treacherous to compacts

Without Natural Affection:
hard-hearted towards kindred

Implacable: unforgiving; will not be appeased

Unmerciful: unfeeling; pitiless; cruel; hard-hearted

Whose mouth is full of cursing and bitterness (Romans 3:14).

Cursing: to pray a curse or calamity to befall someone

Bitterness: sharpness; biting sarcasm (uttered with scorn or contempt)

For ye are yet carnal: for whereas there is among you envying, and strife, and divisions, are ye not carnal, and walk as men? (1 Corinthians 3:3).

Strife: quarrel; wrangling; easily irritated; petulant (sourness of temper; cross; contentious)

Divisions: disunion; the act of dividing, separating, discord

Know ye not that the unrighteous shall not inherit the kingdom of God? Be not deceived: neither fornicators, nor idolaters, nor adulterers, nor effeminate, nor abusers of themselves with mankind, Nor thieves, nor covetous, nor drunkards, nor revilers, nor extortioners, shall inherit the kingdom of God. And such were some of you: but ye are washed, but ye are sanctified, but ye are justified in the name of the Lord Jesus, and by the Spirit of our God" (1 Corinthians 6:9-11)

Idolaters: an image worshipper, idol, images; to idolize money; to idolize children; to idolize a hero

Effeminate: qualities of the female sex; soft or delicate to an unmanly degree; womanish

Abusers of Themselves with Mankind:
a Sodomite; sexual intercourse between men; also between a man and an animal (beastiality)

Drunkards: tipsy; habitually drunk; excessive use of strong liquor

Revilers: abusive; to misuse, insult; contemptuous language

Extortionists: rapacious; disposed or accustomed to seize by force; illegal exaction; taking anything by force, for example, money, articles of value, where none is due

Let all bitterness, and wrath, and anger, and clamour, and evil speaking, be put away from you, with all malice (Ephesians 4:31).

Wrath: violent anger; fury; ire; greatly incensed; rage

Anger: to excite passion or deep displeasure

Clamor: an outcry, shriek, notification; tumult or grief; loud call; a great outcry made by a loud human voice continued or repeated or by a multitude of voices; often expresses complaint and urgent demand; noisy; loud

But fornication, and all uncleanness, or covetousness, let it not be once named among you, as becometh saints; Neither filthiness, nor foolish talking, nor jesting, which are not convenient: but rather giving of thanks. For this ye know, that no whoremonger, nor unclean person, nor covetous man, who is an idolater, hath any inheritance in the kingdom of Christ and of God (Ephesians 5:3-5).

Uncleanness: impurity (the quality - physically or morally); foul; dirty; filthy; indecent; morally impure; foul with sin; squalor

Filthiness: shamefulness; obscenity; shameful; base; vile; without dignity; impure; anything that sullies or defiles the moral character

Foolish Talking:
silly talk; buffoonery (vulgar, coarse, no dignity); heedless (no self respect); shows how foolish a person is

Jesting: obscene jesting; repulsive; impure

Now the works of the flesh are manifest, which are these; Adultery, fornication, uncleanness, lasciviousness, Idolatry, witchcraft, hatred, variance, emulations, wrath, strife, seditions, heresies, Envyings, murders, drunkenness, revellings, and such like: of the which I tell you before, as I have also told you in time past, that they which do such things shall not inherit the kingdom of God (Galatians 5:19-21).

Witchcraft:	medication (pharmacy); by extension magic, sorcery (a drug, spell; giving potion) a druggist (pharmacist or poisoner) by extension a magician
Hatred:	hostility; intense ill will; great dislike; loathe
Variance:	wrangling; contention
Emulations:	jealousy (as of a husband); to be hot; rivalry
Seditions:	disunion; dissension; strife; rebellion; seditious behaviour; an inciter, promoter of discontent
Heresies:	theoretically schismatic: to split, sever, divide; a form of religious worship, discipline or opinion, for example, Acts 5:17; Acts 24:14

Envyings:	ill will (as detraction); jealousy (spite)
Revellings:	a carousal (as if a letting loose); to act wantonly; to feast with loose and clamorous merriment; debauchery, for example, bacchanalian (bacchanal, Bacchus— the god of wine); any orgy of drunkenness and debauchery
And such like:	similar (in appearance or character)

Mortify therefore your members which are upon the earth; fornication, uncleanness, inordinate affection, evil concupiscence, and covetousness, which is idolatry: For which things' sake the wrath of God cometh on the children of disobedience: In the which ye also walked some time, when ye lived in them. But now ye also put off all these; anger, wrath, malice, blasphemy, filthy communication out of your mouth. Lie not one to another, seeing that ye have put off the old man with his deeds (Colossians 3:5-9).

Inordinate Affection:

the lust of desire; pathos: to wound, hurt, to suffer, (pathos is the soul's diseased condition out of which various lusts spring); unlawful or irregular desire for sexual pleasure; desire eagerly pornography, self-sexual satisfaction, etc.; not limited to rules prescribed

Evil Concupiscence:

                        to set the heart upon; a longing, especially for what is forbidden and is evil

Malice: badness; malicious; deliberate intention to injure

Filthy Communication:

                        vile conversation

Lie: to utter an untruth or attempt to deceive by falsehood

He is proud, knowing nothing, but doting about questions and strifes of words, whereof cometh envy, strife, railings, evil surmisings, Perverse disputings of men of corrupt minds, and destitute of the truth, supposing that gain is godliness: from such withdraw thyself" (1 Timothy 6:4-5).

Strifes of Words:

                        disputation about trifles (logo-machies), meaning a fighter about words; a war of words (from this comes envy, strife, railings, evil surmisings)

Evil Surmisings: to think under (privately); i.e.,
     to surmise, conjecture

Perverse Disputings:
     meddlesomeness

> *This know also, that in the last days perilous times shall come. For men shall be lovers of their own selves, covetous, boasters, proud, blasphemers, disobedient to parents, unthankful, unholy, Without natural affection, trucebreakers, false accusers, incontinent, fierce, despisers of those that are good, Traitors, heady, highminded, lovers of pleasures more than lovers of God; Having a form of godliness, but denying the power thereof: from such turn away. For of this sort are they which creep into houses, and lead captive silly women laden with sins, led away with divers lusts, Ever learning, and never able to come to the knowledge of the truth. Now as Jannes and Jambres withstood Moses, so do these also resist the truth: men of corrupt minds, reprobate concerning the faith. But they shall proceed no further: for their folly shall be manifest unto all men, as their's also was"* (2 Timothy 3:1-9).

Lovers of Their Own Selves:
     those who love themselves more

than they ought to, involving conceit and selfishness

Unthankful:	thankless; ungrateful
Unholy:	wicked
Incontinent:	without self-control
Fierce:	savage (extreme unfeeling; brutal cruelty)

Despisers of Those Who Are Good:
hostile to virtue

Traitor:	betrayer, surrender to the enemy
Heady:	rash
High-minded:	Conceited

Paul the Apostle said:

For I am not ashamed of the gospel of Christ: for it is the power [Dunamis] of God unto salvation [rescue or safety; physical or moral health; a deliverer) to every one that believeth; to the Jew first, and also to the Greek (Romans 1:16).

For therein is the righteousness [equity of character or act; innocent, holy, just] of God revealed [disclosed; to take off the cover] from [denoting origin, the point whence motion or action proceed] faith to [indicating the point reached or entered of place, time, purpose] faith: as it is written, The just [innocent, holy] shall live by [the point whence motion or action proceeds] faith (Romans 1:17).

But have renounced [to say off for one-self or disown] the hidden things of dishonesty [concealed; private; inwards; secret; conceal by covering; shame or disgrace; disfigurement; to feel shame for oneself], not walking in craftiness [trickery or sophistry; cunning], nor handling the word of God deceitfully; but by manifestation [exhibition, a bestowment] of the truth commending ourselves to every man's conscience in the sight of God (2 Corinthians 4:2).

But there were false prophets [religious imposters] also among the people, even as there shall be false teachers among you, who privily shall bring in damnable heresies [disunion; sects], even denying [reject, disavow] the Lord that bought them, and bring upon themselves swift destruction. And many shall follow [imitate; obey] their pernicious [destructive] ways; by reason of whom the way of truth [route; journey] shall be evil [defame; blaspheme against God] spoken of. And through covetousness [fraudulency; greediness; desiring more] shall they with feigned [molded; false; fabricated] words make merchandise [trade] of you: whose judgment now of a long time lingereth not, and their damnation slumbereth not. For if God spared [treat leniently] not the angels that sinned, but cast them down to hell [deepest abyss of Hades; to incarcerate in eternal torment], and delivered them into chains [as binding] of darkness [cloudy; as shrouding like a cloud], to be reserved [keeping the eye upon] unto judgment [justice]; And spared [treat leniently] not the old [ancient] world, but saved [preserved] Noah the eighth person, a preacher of righteousness [equitable in character or act; holy; innocent], bringing in the flood upon the world of the ungodly [irreverent]; And turning the cities of Sodom and Gomorrha into ashes condemned [sentenced] them with an overthrow [sentenced], making them an ensample [an exhibit for warning] unto those that after should live ungodly; And delivered just [right as self-evident] Lot, vexed [sore distressed] with the filthy [absence of restraint, excess, indecency] conversation [behaviour] of the wicked (2 Peter 2:1-7).

BIBLIOGRAPHY

Strong, James. *Strong's Exhaustive Concordance of the Bible.* Nashville: Abingdon, 1980.

Vine, W.E. *Vine's Expository Dictionary of Old and New Testament Words.* Iowa Falls, IA: World Bible Publishers, 1981.

Webster's New Dictionary. New York: Publishers Guild, 1955.

Zodhiates, Spiro. *Complete Word Study New Testament with Greek Parallel* (King James Version). Chattanooga, TN: AMG Publishers, 1992.

Zodhiates, Spiro. *Complete Word Study Old Testament* (King James Version). Chattanooga, TN: AMG Publishers, 1994.

ABOUT THE AUTHOR

George LeRoy was born in Ontario, Canada. Upon hearing the message of salvation in his late teens, he became a born-again believer. After receiving the infilling of the Holy Spirit, he left his job in the business world and entered Bible college to prepare himself for pastoral ministry, fulfilling the calling God had placed upon his heart.

After graduation, he entered full-time ministry and was ordained in 1959 with The Assemblies of God, Springfield, Missouri. He encountered, as a pastor, serious family problems in many of the churches he ministered in. At that time, counselling and prayer were extremely helpful in bringing temporary relief to some of the more severe family problems, yet permanent relief for many of the families involved seemed out of reach.

Pastor LeRoy began praying for answers from his Heavenly Father. It was not until 1976 that God, through "Divine Intervention," brought Pastor George into a deliverance ministry. Since that time, he has travelled to many countries of the world, bringing the message of spiritual warfare and deliverance to those who believe and embrace the truth. As God has led, Pastor George and Ruth, his wife of fifty years, have seen God do what no man could do through natural or fleshly means.

I use God's mighty weapons, not those made by men, to knock down the devil's strongholds (2 Corinthians 10:4, TLB).

For the weapons of our warfare are not carnal, but mighty through God, to the pulling down of strong holds (2 Corinthians 10:4).